Let's go to

A road-user education book
Roadwise Educational Publishers

Written by Jean Roberts
Illustrated by Colin Hale

First published in Great Britain 2006 by
5alive Educational Publishers
P O Box 4555
Halesowen
B63 4SY
UK
www.5alive.org.uk

Text Copyright © Jean Roberts 2006
Illustrations Colin Hale
© Roadwise Educational Publishers 2006

British Cataloguing in Publication Data
A Catalogue record for this book is available from the British Library

Printed and bound in Great Britain by Goodman Baylis Ltd

All rights reserved.
No part of this publication may be reproduced, stored in a retrieval system, or transmitted, in any form or by any means, electronic, mechanical, photocopying, recording, scanning or otherwise without the prior written permission of the publisher.

ISBN 0 9524272 3 0

To the carnival!

"Come on," shouted Mum, "do hurry up, Adam."

"Where did you say we were going?" asked Adam.

"We're going to a flower carnival," replied his

Mother.

"A flower carnival? But I don't ------"

It was no use! his stance and face said it all – but he knew he'd be made to go.

"Yes," repeated his Mother, "a flower carnival, and I know that you'll enjoy it, Adam."

"Huh!" sulked Adam, "Ouch, I've got such a pain in my stomach. I think I'm ill! Oh the pain....!"

It was futile to complain. All the family were going, except for Dad who was at work. The carnival was held in another town several miles away - Adam had no idea what a flower carnival was, but he just knew it would be boring. His two sisters seemed keen to go, and he thought it was going to be something for girls and he was being dragged along.

As they got nearer to the 'pick up' point for the coach they could see lots of people already waiting.

"There, I told you that lots of people would be going," said Rachel, laughing at Adam. She got fed up with his complaining when he didn't want to do something. "You'll like it, so stop moaning."

"We'd better cross at the Pelican crossing," interrupted Sara.

The red man was shining so Sara pressed the button.

Adam was daydreaming, dragging his feet as he walked slowly behind them. When he caught up with them he just continued straight out into the road.

"Adam!" shouted his Mother, "Get back on

the pavement." But it was too late. A passing car suddenly swerved to avoid him.

"Phew," sighed Rachel. "Adam, when will you learn, you could have caused an accident."

"Yes," replied his Mother, "if you had been running or the car had been speeding, you might have ended up *under* that car. Just think what the consequences could have been then."

"If there'd been another car coming the other way, the cars might have collided and it would have been all your fault," Sara chipped in.

"Just spend some time thinking about others," shouted Rachel angrily. "Just because you don't want to come. We do - so don't spoil it for us, just because you don't want to go. So stop your sulking."

"And how do you think the driver might be feeling now? Why should he suffer because of your thoughtlessness and lack of responsibility for others," interrupted his mother.

Adam had been rebuked and was by now feeling very sorry for himself and very foolish. He had been planning a last- minute way of saving himself from what he considered would be a day of misery, but now he knew he'd have to go with them. His thoughts were interrupted by a 'bleep, bleep' sound and he looked up to see the green man shining.
"Come on, Adam," prompted Sara, "But we must check the road for ourselves to make sure it is safe for us to cross."

Adam had by now awoken from his daydreaming and he, together with everyone, checked the road for himself.

"Yes it's clear so walk straight across the road, remembering to keep looking and listening as you cross the road, (just in case anything unexpected happens)." Sara repeated what they'd been taught by their parents.

Adam groaned in reply, but he did keep looking and listening all the way across the road. Why, oh why did he have to go?

He began to reflect a little on his stupidity, realising the importance of always being alert and checking the road and waiting for the green man to shine. He certainly didn't want to end up in an accident so he would have to mind his ways every time he crossed the road, and always remember to use the 5 alive code!

While they were waiting for the coach, they talked about the day ahead. They were very glad that the weather was fine and sunny, and the girls spoke quite excitedly about the carnival. They hadn't been before, but they had heard their friends talk about it. Adam was still not convinced and he continued to sulk!

It wasn't long before the coach arrived. The two girls sat by each other and Adam sat with his mother. He wished that Dad had been able to come with them as he felt that he needed a bit of 'male' support - surrounded as he was by all these females!

The coach moved on to the next stopping place. Adam looked out of the window and suddenly noticed his new friend, Ben, in the crowd.
"Ben!" shouted Adam through the window.
"Don't shout so loudly," said his Mother, "and

anyway, he won't hear you through the window. Wait until he gets on the coach, and don't shout right down the bus - wave, call out his name, but don't shout!"

Adam had by now clambered past his mother and was in the aisle – "Ben!" he half screamed, "come down here!"

Ben made his way down to the back of the coach and the two boys sat together.

"What are you doing going to a flower carnival Ben? I've been dragged here under protest!"

"Under protest? but it's fantastic - haven't you ever been before?" asked Ben.

"Err – no," replied Adam rather surprised at Ben's enthusiasm.

"Oh but it's great," said Ben, "all those floats covered in flower heads, and clowns, old bikes and all sorts of things."

"Really?" said Adam still quite confused. Perhaps he might enjoy it after all?

Carnival Queens

Ben and Adam chatted endlessly and by the time they reached 'carnival town' Adam was nearly as enthusiastic as everyone else.

"Right," said the coach driver, "everyone needs to be back here at 5pm prompt. The way to the carnival is down that road," (he pointed the way). "Just follow the crowds."

The coach had parked on a road right by a church and there were streams of people all walking in one direction.

"Now, I don't want to lose you," said Adam's mother, "we'll just have to keep each other in sight, but if ever we were to get parted then the name of the road is Buttercup Lane and the church is called St Paul's. Wait, I'll write down the name on this piece of paper, put it in your pocket and keep it safe, just in case you need it."

"Don't panic! I've got my mobile," piped up Ben.

They were jostled in the crowd, there were so many people. Adam was amazed. He still couldn't quite take in all the enthusiasm! The town was alive with a buzz of excitement.

There were market stalls selling all sorts of things, the girls found one selling different bracelets, necklaces and rings, and right next to that stall was one selling model aeroplanes and ships. Adam had made a model aeroplane and soon he and Ben were engrossed in looking at all the models on display.

The girls were trying on some bracelets, there was just so much choice. Everyone wanted to buy something. They had their pocket money with them but their mothers said they should leave buying anything until they came back as they might see something better, and in any case they didn't want to carry things with them all day! They all protested, but their mothers' minds were made up. However, Adam, Ben,

Rachel and Sara had a good idea of what they wanted to buy from the stall on their way back. They just hoped that in the crowd they would be able to find it again!

They saw a clown selling programmes and they decided to get one so that they would know what time things were happening. They read that the procession took place all day, part in the morning and part in the afternoon.

They were again carried along with the crowds. The streets were thick with people all making their way to watch the procession. From the air it must have looked like an army of ants racing to an open jam jar! Rachel spotted a small space on the very wide grass verge at the side of the road and as it was very hot they sat down and had some of the drink they had brought with them.

They were just finishing, when Adam shouted, "I can hear drums."

A band soon came into view.

"Oh look," said Sara, "the band are all dressed up as elves."

They all had pointed red hats and blue, red or green tunic tops, with red or yellow trousers. They looked very colourful and bright. There were all sizes of drums and some other unusual instruments. Adam, Ben, Rachel and Sara were all stamping their feet in time with the drums and swaying in time to the music. It was such fun! Even Adam had to admit that he was enjoying himself!

Following the band was a very spectacular float, a carriage completely made of flower petals, except for the wheels, which as it came closer, were seen to be made out of polystyrene.

"I thought at first it was an old carriage

'dressed up' but I see that it must have been made using a framework," said Ben thoughtfully. He was always keen to know how something was made or how something worked.

Inside was sitting a very pretty girl who didn't look much older than themselves.
"Who's that?" asked Ben.
"I expect it will be the carnival queen," answered his Mother.

The carnival queen waved to them. She looked so lovely, just like a film star in her pink satin dress and deep purple sash.
"I wish I were sitting there," whispered Sara, "she looks so pretty."
"You'd look every bit as pretty as she does," responded her mother encouragingly.

Sara gazed at the Carnival Queen as she went

past them and wondered if ever she could be a queen for a day? She imagined herself dressed up in a lovely long gown, sitting in the carriage with people waving at her. She was very happy in her own little paradise when all of a sudden she was brought back to reality!

I can hear a steam engine!" shouted Adam.
They all craned their necks to see what was approaching them.
The 'steam engine' was hooting as it travelled slowly along the road. It was all decorated with flowers. Ben and Adam stared hard. The wheels were going round and round, so was it a real steam engine? They had already been fooled by the Carnival Queen's carriage! The sound was definitely the noise of a steam engine, but no steam was billowing out of its funnel. Then they solved the problem: the

wheels were turning, but were not touching the ground, there wasn't any steam and so they concluded that the sound must be from a recording.

Behind the engine was a portly gentleman trying to keep up with the float, and chasing him were lots of boys and girls all dressed up and waving to the crowds. They clapped and shouted to tell the man to hurry up, but he didn't seem able to run very fast!

"What's that?" asked Rachel, I can see people floating in the sky!"

Riding high

They peered into the distance. Ghostly figures seemed to hover in the sky.

"So that's what they are," laughed Rachel, "not angels or ghosts but only humans!"

"They are just so high," gasped Sara in

amazement.

The riders of the 'penny farthings' towered above everyone.

And then they saw more and more bicycles, - and tricycles.

There were bicycles and tricycles of all shapes and sizes, ridden by children and adults. Some of the adults seemed quite old.

"I wonder if they had them from new," wondered Sara as she snapped some more photos.

"Don't be so cheeky, Sara. Even the oldest person isn't that old!" laughed her Mother.

"Wow, look at that little boy on his tricycle," said Rachel.

"Doesn't look very comfortable," laughed Ben, "it looks as though it has hard wheels, and..., oh, look the pedals are on the front wheel."

"Is that what's called a bone-shaker?" asked Sara looking at another bicycle. "It looks very hard to ride, with those large wooden wheels."

"Yes, I think it must be," said Adam's Mother. "It does look most uncomfortable, but the man riding it is managing to smile!"

"I wish we could ride some of these bicycles," said Ben. "I fancy a 'penny farthing'."

"How would you climb up to get onto it?" laughed his Mother.

"And I'd like to ride a little tricycle like that boy there," said Adam, " it looks so cute!"

"Perhaps there's a museum where you can try out these veteran cycles," said Ben's mother. "I'll make enquiries when we get home."

"Do you think they would come to our school?" asked Sara. "We could learn about the changing shape of the bicycle, and experience the changes for ourselves."

"Good idea," agreed Adam. "Mrs Williams will arrange it for us I'm sure."

"Mrs Williams will really thank me for bringing you here!" said Adam's mother.
"I'd really like to have a go on those bicycles," remarked Sara already picturing herself on one.

A man standing next to them overheard what they said and told them about the Road-user Activity Centre where they could ride real veteran bicycles and special child-size ones too. He told them that it was just off junction 5 of the motorway. He had taken his children there many times from when they were quite young, and even now they were much older they still opted for a visit to the centre in the school holidays. There was just so much to do; something for all ages and interests, with activities for pedestrians, cyclists and car drivers.

"Must be worth going to," thought Ben.

"That's another trip to do in the holidays," replied Rachel gleefully.

Ben was studying another tricycle as it went past them. "That tricycle also has its large wheels at the front," noticed Ben with surprise. "I wonder how it works?"

Ben was fascinated with the variety of cycles. Some tricycles had large wheels either side of the person who sat in the middle; some had two extremely large wheels at the front and a very tiny wheel at the back, while others had quite a large wheel at the front and two larger wheels on the back.

Ben was not quite sure how one lady steered the tricycle as there wasn't even a handlebar! "Which bike would you like to ride, Ben?"

"I think I'd like to try one of the cycles where the person sits in the middle, but I'd have to be careful I didn't fall off as there aren't any handlebars to hold. So, no, perhaps I'll change my mind and go for a penny farthing, if I can climb up!"

"That sounds even more tricky to ride!" mused

Rachel.

"Perhaps someone in school would help you make replicas of the cycles?" said Mother, tongue in cheek, visualising Mrs Williams's reaction.

"Well, you seem as though you'll look forward to going back to school. Lessons could take on a new interest!" added Ben's mother.

"Were the bicycles like that when you were our age?" asked Ben ignoring his Mother's comment.

"Now how old do you think we are!" laughed his Mother. "We might seem ancient, but the bicycles we rode were really quite similar to the ones you have."

"I think I'll make a scrapbook of old bikes," said Sara. "I've already got several photos today and I can find more bikes on the Internet and label them in my scrapbook, writing down where I saw them."

"That's a good idea. I think I'll make a scrapbook too," echoed Ben, "and I'll also include notes about how they were made."

"Those will be really useful scrapbooks and ones you may well want to keep for a long time, maybe even show your own children and then they will probably ask if you rode bikes like that!" laughed Ben's mother getting her own back!

"Why are they called 'scrapbooks' when you usually keep them?" asked Ben.

"Oh, more questions," remarked his Mother. "I really don't know the true answer, Ben. I think people used to put little bits and pieces into a scrapbook, but why don't you look it up? I think we may see more bikes this afternoon, so you'll be able to take more photos for your scrapbook."

As the next part of the procession was to be held in the afternoon they decided to wander and perhaps see some of the attractions listed in the programme guide.

Meeting toad

They were walking along when suddenly Rachel shouted, "Look over there, it's a toad!" Just over the road on the other side of the river was indeed a rather large toad. They wanted to get a better look at it so they needed to cross the road.

They looked for the safest place to cross the road. There wasn't a Pelican or Zebra crossing in sight, in fact there wasn't a designated crossing place in view, so they chose a safe place not far from where they were and walked to it.

Rachel and Sara, Ben and Adam stood by each other. They waited on the pavement and looked this way and that for traffic and saw only one vehicle approaching, a bicycle. The cyclist rang his bell and they waited until he had passed them and kept looking and listening.

They kept looking and listening as they waited on the pavement and as there wasn't another vehicle in sight they walked straight across the road, remembering to keep looking and listening as they went safely to the other side.

'Toad' was right in front of them, a very large smart looking toad! His head was made out of laurel leaves and the rest of him was made out of tulips. His jacket was red, his feet were black and his legs yellow and white tulips. In his hand he held a fishing rod.

As they examined 'Toad,' the vast number of flower heads needed just to make one small character amazed them, and they looked forward to the afternoon when they would see some really large flower floats.

Ben's mother explained to them that lots of bulbs were grown in the area, and that the flower heads had to be cut off so that the bulbs would swell and grow large. It was a long time ago when it was decided to use the 'waste' flower heads and have a special event where they could use them. The idea of a carnival was born.

"But wouldn't the petals go limp and withered?" questioned Rachel.

"Yes, I believe that lots of people all help for just a few days before the carnival, putting on the thousands of flower heads," responded Ben's mother.

"I guess we'd be allowed a week off school to help," muttered Adam, always keen to avoid the classroom!

"But the frames must take much longer to make?" asked Ben thoughtfully.

"Oh yes," replied his Mother," I believe they begin soon after one carnival with ideas for the next year, and then work begins on the construction for the floats many months before the carnival. It is a year long commitment and it is all done voluntarily."

"I understand that the carnival has grown so large that nowadays they combine paper flowers with the real ones, as they need so many," said Adam's mother. She told them that they would see thousands and thousands of flower heads later in the day.

They were distracted from 'Toad' to the river where a small 'boat' was coming into view.

"It looks rather like a canoe, doesn't it, but it isn't a canoe. What's it called?" asked Adam.

Sara piped up, "It's a coracle, we learned about those at school."

"There's another coracle," said Ben looking farther up the river.

Several coracles came past them. One advertised that children could have a 'ride' in them and should meet at the Coracle Centre down the road.

Ben, Adam, Sara and Rachel all wanted to have a ride in one! Sara was very keen to have a ride as she had made a very small replica of a coracle at school, but had been away from school when a visitor had brought in a real coracle to show the pupils. As there was some time before the main carnival, they decided to go straight away to the Coracle Centre.

They followed the signs to the Centre and spotted it on the other side of the road. They looked for the safest place to cross the road. Ben pointed towards a Zebra crossing.

They all made their way to the crossing and

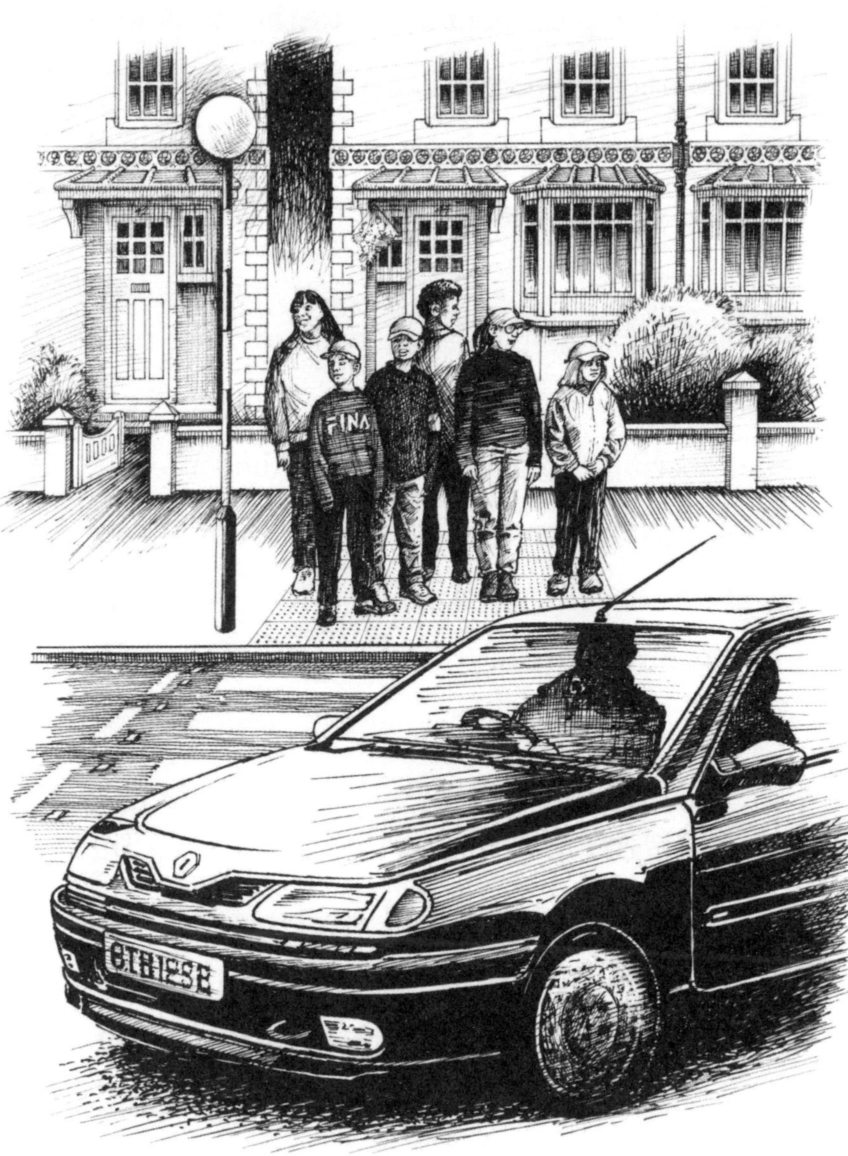
FINA

stood on the pavement near to the kerb and kept looking and listening for traffic.

"I wish someone would stop and let us cross the road," said Adam getting frustrated.

"If I had a 'Lollipop pole,' I'd walk into the road and stop the traffic myself!" laughed Ben, remembering the time when they had been in the playground and taken turns with a lollipop pole to cross children over the 'road'. They kept looking and listening, hoping that the traffic would soon stop.

Just then a car stopped. They looked and listened again and waited until the car on the other side of the road had stopped too before they began to walk straight across the crossing, looking and listening as they went, just in case anything unexpected happened.

They arrived at the Coracle Centre but discovered that lots of other people also had the same idea. They saw some coracles upturned on the bank, and others were being carried on the backs of adults towards the water. Children were already in some of the coracles, in a specially constructed pool, cut off from the main lake leading into the river. They stood at the end of a long queue waiting their turn.

After their mothers had paid for their tickets, they were directed along one of the many paths leading to the different jetties around the large pool. There were boards telling them about the history of coracles, how they were made and how to use them.

Moving past the boards they were met by a trainer who gave them each a paddle and showed them how to use it. The paddle was

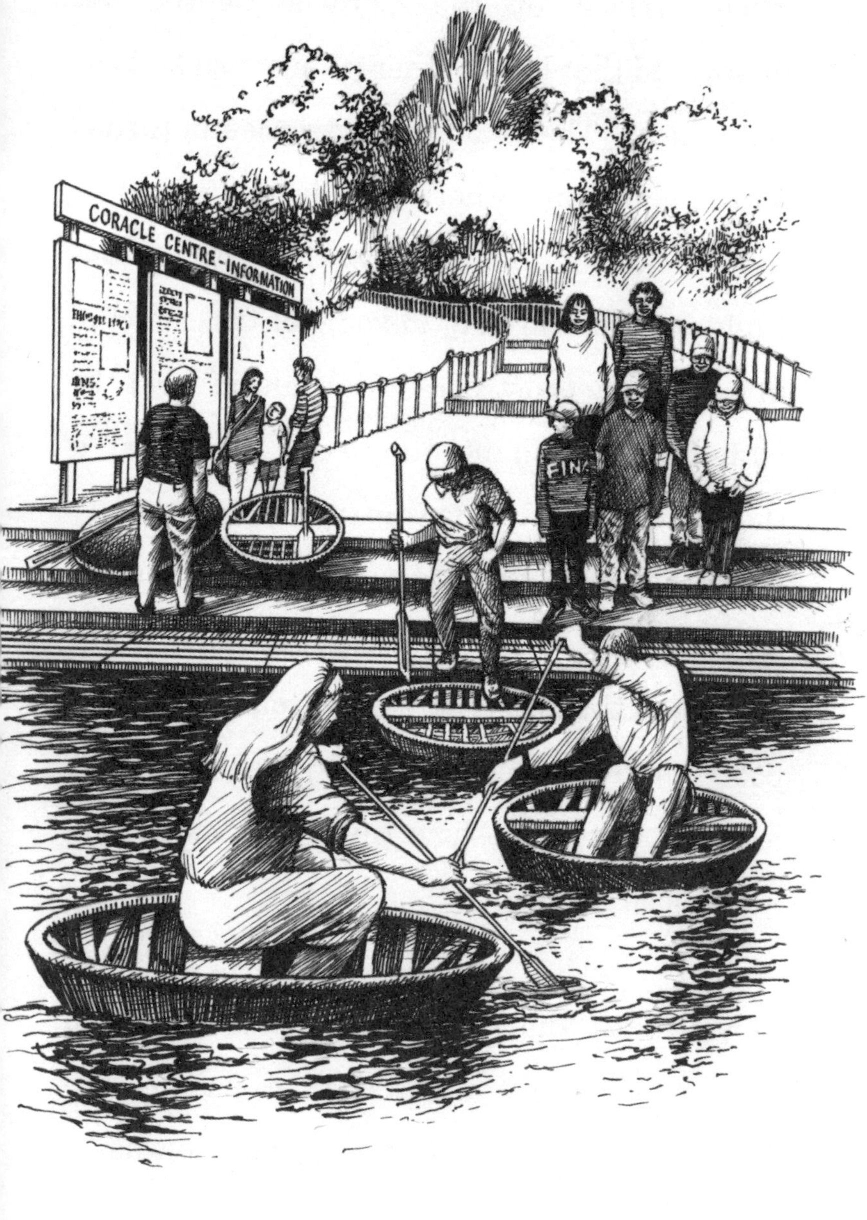
CORACLE CENTRE-INFORMATION

quite long and took time learning how to control it. They kept practising with their paddles while they waited for their turn.

A trainer went in the coracle with the younger children but Ben and his group were given several more instructions and then allowed to go in a coracle on their own. Just getting in and out of a coracle was not easy as one sat on a kind of bench which was level with the top of the coracle! It felt very strange at first, but there were plenty of trainers walking around in the water helping the children.

Ben and Rachel soon got the idea of what to do with their paddle, but Adam, in his usual, 'I know how to do it, I don't need any help' attitude, was surprised to find just how difficult it was to manoeuvre the little boat. He began to get frustrated and was furiously moving his paddle. He was wobbling all over the place, and even attempted to stand up, however, inevitably, the next minute he was in the water holding his paddle aloft! One of the adults soon spotted him and helped him to the side. Everyone was laughing, but Adam did not see the funny side!

Fortunately for him his Mother always carried everything for any emergency and she gave him some clothes to change into. Adam said that he didn't want to have another go but one of the trainers came up to Adam and encouraged him not to give up. He showed Adam again how to manage the paddle and when Adam was in the coracle, the trainer stayed right there with him until he had got the idea of what to do and was able to progress forwards more easily. Adam's pride was indeed rather dented, but soon he was progressing well, and his beaming face was proof that he had recovered! Even people on the side and in the other coracles began to clap him and he soon felt like a hero! Both Mothers were taking photographs and with all the talk about scrapbooks they thought they might make one about the whole day! Perhaps later Adam would see the funny side, with a before and after photo!

They were all enjoying this new experience and were very sad when it came to an end. Before they left the centre they were given leaflets about courses for children and adults: apparently they could even make their own coracle on one of the courses! Both Mothers looked at the leaflet and agreed that they would bring the children over for a half day course during the school holidays and with that promise they all went away contented and excited!

The girls kept on at Adam about his falling into the water, but his Mother told them to let it drop as no one is perfect, and they may need some support one day.

"It is much nicer to be kind and thoughtful rather than to keep teasing and being horrid!" said Mother sternly.

It was now the girls who felt rather subdued on returning to join the main procession.

The clowns

They positioned themselves so that they would have a good view of the procession. As they were waiting, an ice-cream seller came cycling along and stopped by them. Everyone thought they'd like an ice lollipop on such a warm day.

"It's a good thing that we've got our caps on," said Ben.

"Yes, and our sun lotion," agreed Rachel.

People were sitting on the kerb, others were standing, and several people had brought chairs, probably they'd been before and knew just how tiring it could be standing for so long.

By now Adam was beginning to feel that the day was proving to be more interesting than he had ever thought possible! He was actually getting excited at what else he might see and experience!

"I can hear another band coming," said Adam turning his head to listen to the music.

"I wonder what these people will be wearing?" wondered Ben.

They didn't have long to wait.

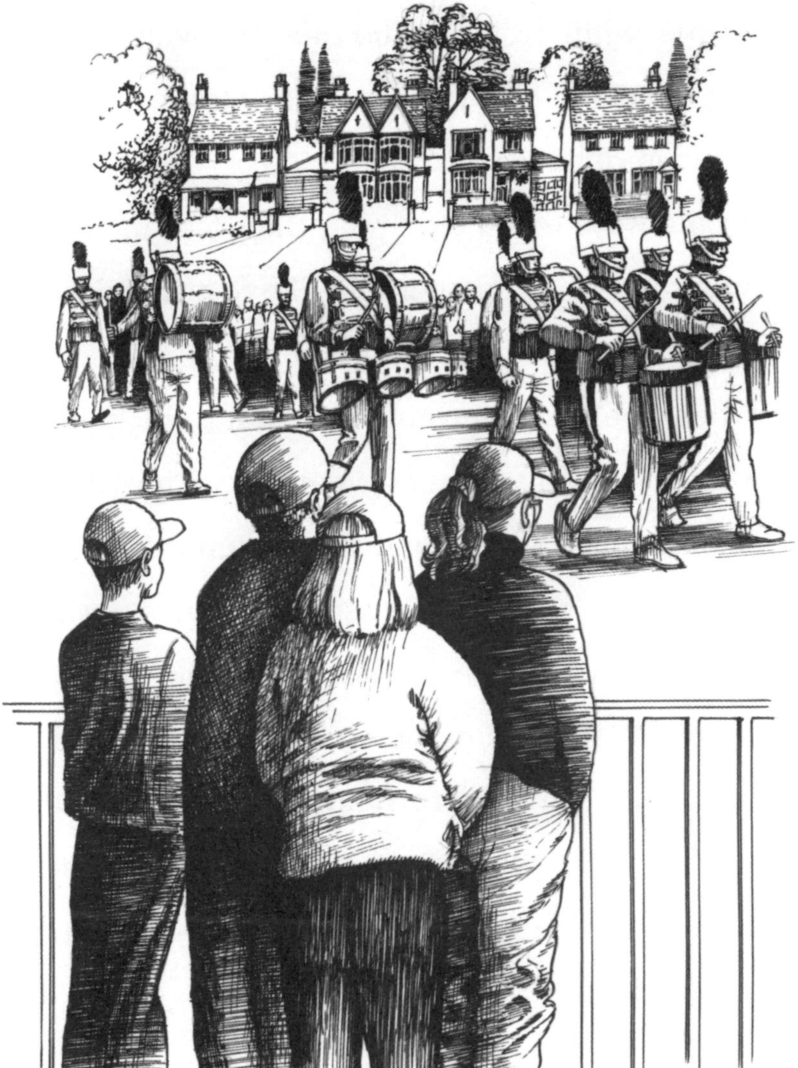

They were wearing blue jackets with white stripes; white trousers and their tall white hats had a mass of blue feathers. They looked like a regimental band.

People were again stamping their feet in time with the music. They would like to have joined in and marched with the group.

When the parade came to a halt, the band would walk in various formations. First they went into two lines and then changed sides. Next they went into a spiral following the leader. When the leader was right in the middle he turned around and led the band back out of the circle returning to their original position. By the time this was complete the parade moved on again and the blue and white band was gone.

"When I get back to school I'm going to suggest

to Mrs Williams that we go into a spiral and out again as we leave the hall and go to our class," said Ben.

"Yes," replied Adam, "and I want to be the leader. It would be much more fun than just having to walk out of the hall in a straight line."

"You'd have to practise well and be organised, otherwise I can hear Mrs Williams complaining that it took you all morning to return to your classrooms," laughed Ben's Mother.

"I think school could be much more fun, using different ways of returning to class," said Adam.

By now he could see himself proudly leading the whole school in marching activities!

There followed a group of girls twirling ribbons into the air high above their heads and making large circles. Others had hoops and were rolling the hoops ahead of them. Then came a group of girls marching. One girl had a drum and others had different instruments, but something else caught their eye.

There they were, two very tall clowns walking along the road, with other ones juggling and generally 'clowning' around! The tall clowns had a bucket attached to each leg about knee height, and as they walked children were throwing money into the buckets.
"Quick, give us some money!" said Adam.
They all threw some pennies into the buckets.
"What an aim!" said Ben proudly.
The buckets were rather large with sloping sides and it really wasn't difficult to succeed. However, there were some clowns who weren't very tall and who were very quick at retrieving

any dropped coins.

One clown had found an easy way to travel. He was sitting in a rickshaw being pulled by another clown. Every time the clown stopped and refused to go any farther, he would stand up in the rickshaw and get out a 'whip' (made of balloons) and would beat the other clown until he began to pull the rickshaw once again. Sometimes he would shower the clown with what looked like a bucket of water and sometimes the crowd became his target too!

Another clown came hurtling into view performing cartwheels and then he would leap frog over another clown. This started one of them to give chase ending up with a water fight involving each other and the crowds. These two clowns were always up to something! They shadowed two of the children in the parade who were juggling and when they said 3-2-1 they took over the juggling from the children. When they repeated 3-2-1 the children took over again!

Some clowns who were on unicycles found themselves being chased by these two! At last they caught up and helped each other climb onto the shoulders of those on the unicycles and wave to the crowd from a great height. One of the children threw some balls for the clowns to juggle with, so there were these two clowns juggling while standing on the shoulders of another clown who were riding unicycles!
There followed other clowns, more young children who were juggling and some who were walking on stilts. Two children were riding unicycles looking very confident. They were such a colourful and happy group.

"I wonder what will come next?" asked Ben, hardly able to contain his excitement.

Along came an enormous limousine – all done in tulip heads with huge 'potato shaped people' sitting inside.

"I wonder if they are advertising potatoes?" grinned Ben. "I guess they grow a lot around here. Maybe our potato crisps begin their life right here!"

There were all kinds of floats, and in one of the open top vintage buses was yet another clown who kept ringing the bell and running up and down the stairs, shouting and waving to everyone!

They all liked the clowns and were sad to see them finally move on.

"Wow eee," exclaimed Adam, "just look over there."

"Just look at the size of that pineapple," said

Rachel pointing to the next float.

"And the oranges and strawberries," said Ben, "they are so large!"

"And the banana!" piped up Adam.

It looked as though the float had just arrived from the tropics; only the fruit had grown enormously in size! And yet it was all made from tulip heads!

"Just as well they don't have to go under any bridges," smiled Sara, "as they would get stuck!"

The fruit really were enormous, and the flower heads were obviously real as the fragrance perfumed the air.

A very special float!

"Oh look, there is a float with a Lollipop person," said Rachel.

"There are children standing looking as though they are waiting to cross the road," added Ben.

"Oh yes," said Adam, "and there's also a Zebra

crossing and a book is open at the back of the float."

"They are singing a song. Do you recognise it?" asked Adam.

"Why, it's 'The Road Crossing Song' we learnt in Mr Hazel's class," said Ben.

On the front of the float, in flowers were the words, 'Wait until the road is clear. Keep looking and listening', and on the side of the float were the words 'Look and listen as you go, safe across the road'.

They joined in with the song. The Lollipop person on the float acted as conductor, leading the children and encouraging the crowds to sing along with them.

Some children were walking behind the float and they were dressed up as different kinds of vehicles, tractors, lorries and cars made out of

STOP
Look and listen as you go, safe across the road
Wait until the road is clear.
Keep looking and listening.

cardboard. Some adults were dressed up as 'Lollipop' persons, Pelican lights and Belisha Beacons. One 'Pelican light' came towards them. "Press the button," ordered a voice. Rachel pressed the button and watched as the red man stopped shining and the green man shone, accompanied by the normal 'bleep, bleep' sounds. Underneath the button was a little drawer that opened when the green man shone. Out came a bookmark for Rachel. Now everyone wanted a go! Ben received a Belisha beacon-shaped pencil, Adam had a rubber and Sara had a pencil sharpener.

"I think they could have these at all crossings," said Rachel, "then people might wait for the green man to shine and not go across the road before!"

Some people were giving out leaflets. "If you

answer the questions correctly you can win a half price ticket to the Road-user Activity Centre."

"That's the place that man mentioned," shouted Adam excitedly. "Definitely a place to be visited."

In fact they all liked the idea of visiting the centre, so they each took a leaflet and decided to fill it in when they returned home as there was too much going on right now.

Behind the children, who were dressed up as vehicles, was another Lollipop lady. Mothers and young children were with her and every time the procession stopped she would shout, "Wait there on the pavement, children," and put her hand out to stop them. When the procession began to move on again, she would move forward (with the children still standing where they were) and say, "Cross now children," and allow the children to move past in front of her.

Someone came along selling very large 'pencils' in the shape of a lollipop pole - just like the one Mrs Jones used outside their school. There were also lots of different coloured balloons for sale. On each balloon were the words, 'Look and listen as you go, safe across the road'. Ben and Sara each wanted a large coloured balloon, but Adam and Rachel chose the 'pencils'. The 'pencils' were as tall as they were and Adam secretly decided he could use it to stop the traffic. He also thought he'd cause much amusement in class when he attempted to write with it!

They began to search their pockets for their purses, but their Mothers said they would treat

Look and listen as you go safe across the road
STOP
Look and listen as you go, as safe across the road
STOP

them. They proudly waved their balloons and pencils around.

As the next float came towards them Adam walked into the road to stop the parade, using his 'lollipop pole'. Everyone stopped, and several other children went into the road and held up their 'pencils' too! Then from nowhere, a clown appeared. He crept up from behind and sprayed water on the children! Everyone laughed. He gave the children some sweets and took one of the 'Lollipops' from them, proudly held it up above his head and held out his other hand indicating to the children to return to their places! It was great fun and all of them were really enjoying themselves.

There were several more floats and then the procession came to an end. The crowds swarmed into the road filling all the available space. There were just so many people. Somehow Adam and Ben became separated from the rest of the group!

They were just taken along by the crowd. It was impossible to stop. Adam's Mother shouted to them to meet them at the coach, but it was no use, they were soon some distance from them.

The crowd took them in the direction of the coracles, but both Ben and Adam knew that wasn't the way to the coach.

Getting lost

All of a sudden the crowd seemed to disappear, a bit like being in a traffic jam on the motorway, when, without warning, the traffic clears and you wonder why you were held up.

"Where are they all?" asked Adam.

"I don't know, I was just thinking the same thing myself," replied Ben a little scared. "I think we're lost!"

"Well, we may be lost, but we know where we want to go," said Adam taking charge of the situation. "I've got a piece of paper somewhere in this pocket, and it tells us the name of the road where the coach will be. Anyway, you've got your 'phone."

Ben brightened up at the thought that they weren't going to be lost forever! Suddenly his mouth dropped open. "That's OK,.... only ...I ...forgot to get Sara's number and Mum hasn't got her 'phone with her," replied Ben rather sheepishly. "Still your Mum wrote down the time and place, didn't she?"

Adam struggled to find the scrap of paper.

"Here it is," said Adam. "Five o clock at Buttercup Lane - opposite St Paul's church. What's the time now?"

"It's nearly three thirty," replied Ben.

"Well, we won't find them again in all the crowds so we might as well enjoy ourselves," said Adam confidently.

They were just thinking about what to do when they spotted a rather unusual Pelican crossing: they went to investigate.

The red man was shining but there was something strange, he was completely made of flowers. Ben pressed the button: amazingly, the green man shone and there was the 'bleep, bleep' sound. They stood on the pavement looking and listening for traffic. The road was clear and safe for them to cross. They looked and listened again and as it was still safe they walked straight across the road, remembering to keep looking and listening as they crossed to the other side. They inspected the 'flower' Pelican.

"Cool," said Ben.

"They certainly have plenty of flower heads around here," responded Adam.

"They must grow millions of bulbs to have all these flower heads: tulips, daffodils, hyacinths and lots more that I don't recognise. I quite like the fragrance. I think I shall plant some in our garden this year to remind me of our special day," said Ben.

"I think I shall plant a mini zebra crossing in our garden," mused Adam already planning where it should be. He also secretly thought that Mrs Williams could help them plant a Zebra crossing in the school grounds. It could be a great safety feature and reminder to the pupils to look for a designated crossing place to cross the road – just as long as no one trod on it!

As they walked along the pavement they could hear voices. They hadn't gone more than a few metres when something caught Ben's eye.

The very special float was there right in front of them. There were crowds of people everywhere. They couldn't remember seeing so many people even a few minutes ago when they were admiring the Pelican. The children and adults who had been on the float were still laughing and playing with their 'lollipop' sticks, and the people dressed up as Pelicans and Belisha Beacons were making everyone obey them. Adam and Ben decided to join in.

The Lollipop person was getting the children to

wait on the pavement with her. When the road was clear of traffic she walked into the middle of the road, held up the 'Lollipop stick' and put her other hand out to her side informing the child drivers (still dressed up as vehicles) that they must stop. Then she said to the children on the pavement, 'Cross now, children'. Ben and Adam joined the group and, having checked the road for themselves, they crossed the road with the Lollipop person, remembering to keep looking and listening as they walked straight across the road.

One of the clowns came up to Ben. He had a clipboard and pen and asked Ben some questions. "Why do you stay on the pavement?" asked the clown.

"Because we must wait until the Lollipop person walks into the road and stops the

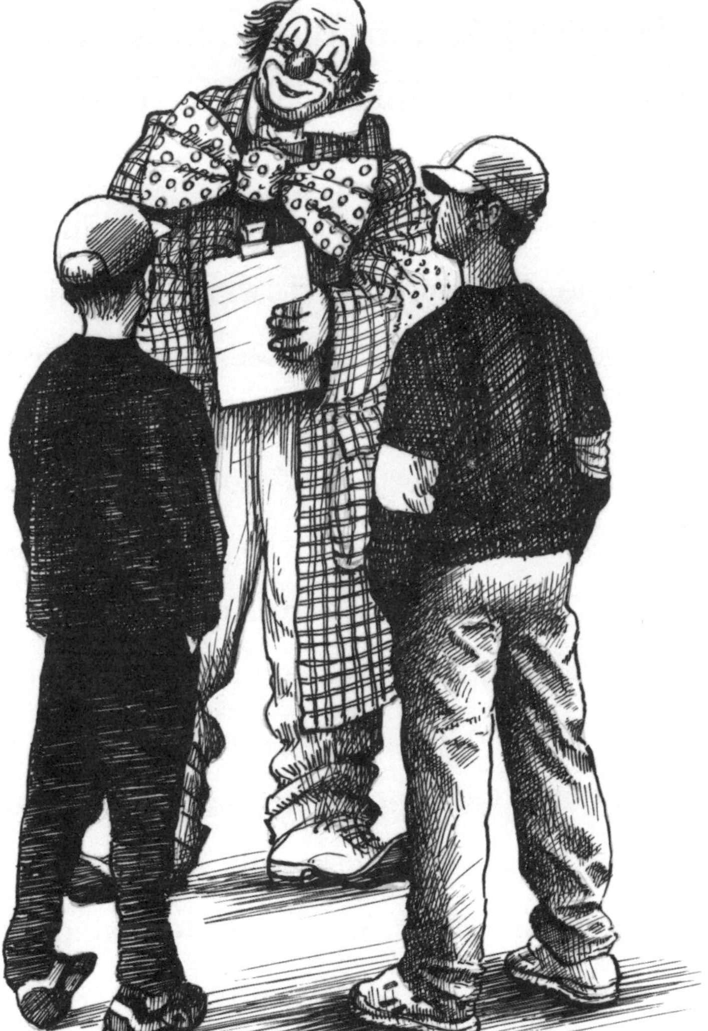

traffic," replied Ben.

"Well done!" said the clown. "Now when the Lollipop person walks into the road, what should you do?"

"Wait patiently on the pavement looking and listening for traffic and waiting until the Lollipop person says, "Cross now, children," said a confident Ben.

"You are doing very well," said the clown, "I have just two more questions. What must you do before and as you are crossing the road?

"Oh I know that one," piped up Adam unable to keep quiet any longer. "You must always keep looking and listening before you begin to cross the road and when safe, walk straight across the road remembering to keep looking and listening, just in case anything unexpected happens."

"What do you mean by something unexpected?"

questioned the clown.

"Well, a pedal cyclist or car driver might suddenly appear and not stop, and could come and run you over – if you weren't looking and didn't move out of the way," replied Adam with an air of superior knowledge.

"Excellent. I really am impressed," said the clown. "Last question. Can you tell me the direction you walk – at an angle or straight across the road?"

"You walk straight across. That is the shortest way to the other side. Roads can be dangerous places and so we need to be sensible and as safe as possible," replied Ben.

The clown held up his hands to attract attention.

"Hi everyone. Come and meet two smart boys who if they behave on the roads as they've just told me they should, they will always be safe when crossing roads," shouted the clown.

All the other children gathered round Adam and Ben.

"Come up onto the float so that everyone can see you," encouraged the clown.

They walked up onto the float. Everyone's eyes were on them. Adam and Ben felt like celebrities. A very tall clown crept up behind them and showered glitter on them from his huge watering can! Then everyone was asked to be quiet as the other clown spoke.

"These two lads have answered my questions brilliantly and as a reward they will be given two tickets for the National Road-user Activity Centre. Let's give them three cheers. Hip hip, hooray! Hip hip, hooray! Hip hip, hooray!" The clown then handed them their tickets.

Wait until the road is clear.
Keep looking and listening.

Everyone clapped and shouted. Ben and Adam felt rather dazed. Then a photographer from the local paper came to take pictures of them and asked where they were from and how they'd heard about the carnival. (Adam refrained from saying that he hadn't wanted to come!)

After all the excitement, Adam and Ben came back to reality and suddenly realised that they should think about making their way back to the coach.

"Remember to buy a local paper on your way home," shouted the photographer as Ben and Adam began to walk away.

The coach. Now where was it?

Fame!

Adam got out the piece of paper with the name of the road where the coach would be picking them up.

"I suppose we'd better begin to find our way there?" said Ben reluctantly. It had all been so exciting that neither of the boys had come back down to earth.

"Oh, but I think we've just got time to see the model aeroplane stall," said Adam.

"If you can find it!" replied Ben looking towards the crowds in the town and wondering if they would ever find the coach, let alone the model stall.

"Well it was in the road near the church, so if we ask someone where Buttercup Lane is, we shall pass by the model stall," said Adam confidently.

"What a bright spark you are," replied Ben admiringly.

"Look, there's a policeman," stated Adam, "let's ask him the way."

They walked up to the policeman who pointed in the direction of Buttercup Lane.

"Thank you," said Adam to the policeman.

They walked along the pavement.

In the distance they could see lots of people all bending.

"I wonder if they are doing their exercises," laughed Ben.

As they got nearer they could tell that they were putting flower heads into the holes of coloured plastic sheeting laid out on the ground.

"They're making a flower mosaic," said Adam in amazement.

The design was painted onto the background – rather like painting by colours. They spotted a mosaic of a Lollipop person with the Lollipop pole and two children walking across the road, heads turned to face the traffic. The words underneath were 'Keep looking and listening as you cross the road (just in case anything unexpected happens)'. Adam and Ben decided to spend a few minutes putting in some flower heads.

"Wow, we really must go to the coach now," exclaimed Ben looking at his watch.

They stood up, admired their contribution to the mosaic and then reluctantly turned in the direction of Buttercup Lane.

"There's the model stall," said Adam pointing ahead. "Let's run across the road."

"No," said Ben. "We must always look for the safest place to cross the road, and there is a Zebra crossing, so we must walk to it and cross the road there.

Remember the tickets we've won? We must always put into practice what we said *every* time we cross the road. I really am surprised at you as only this morning I heard that you

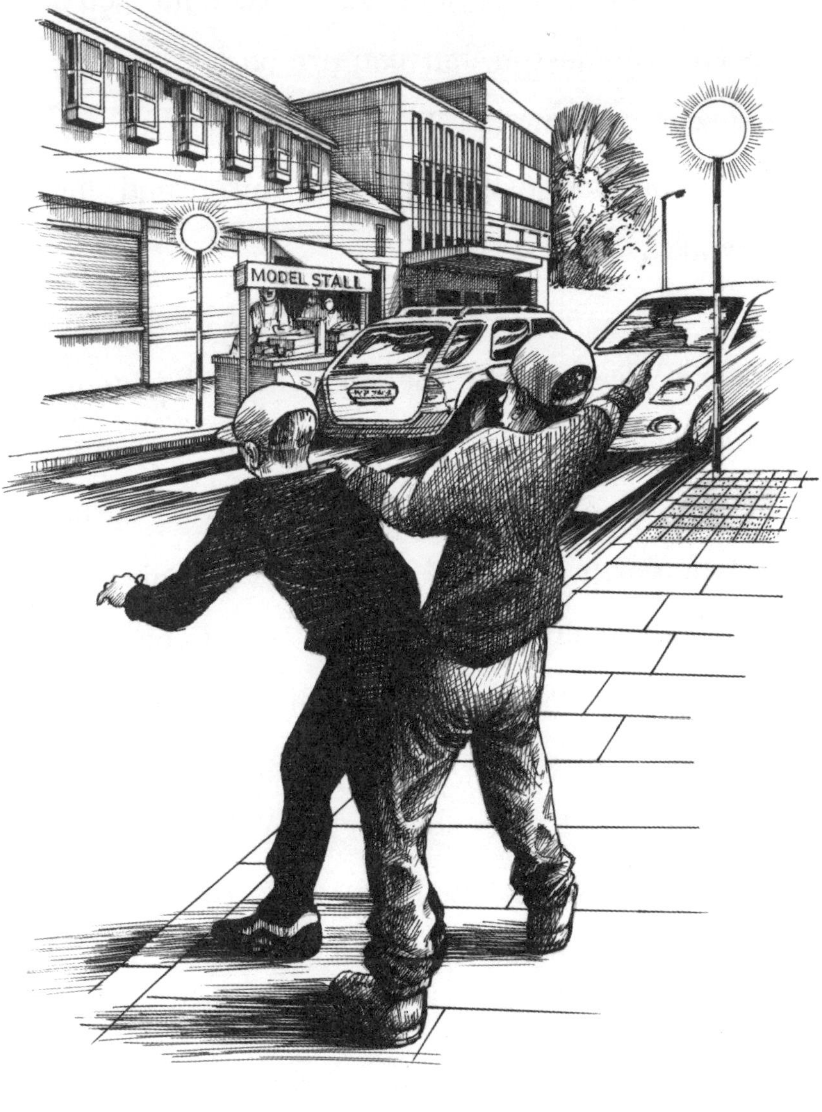
MODEL STALL

nearly had an accident and I thought you'd learnt your lesson, but you are back into your old ways. Grow up, Adam, and take crossing the road seriously. I want my friend for always!"

People seemed to be crossing the road everywhere except on the Zebra crossing. Motorists were hooting their horns continuously. Ben and Adam wisely walked to the Zebra crossing. They stood on the pavement looking and listening for traffic. When the cars had stopped they checked the road again. It was safe for them to cross the road and even though by now there were several people on the crossing, Ben and Adam both remembered to keep looking both ways and listening as they crossed the road, just in case anything unexpected happened.

They were soon at the model stall. It had so many models they would like to have bought, but the money they had left would only buy one small one. At last they had each decided what to buy and proudly handed over their money, keeping the boxes close to themselves as they walked along Buttercup Lane.

"Where's a newsagent's shop so we can buy a paper?" wondered Ben.

They looked around. There was one just ahead of them. As they approached they noticed the headlines, there they were right on the front page! They dashed into the shop and bought a copy, asking the newsagent to look at the photo on the front! He looked at the paper and then at them, his glasses almost fell off his nose!

"Why that's you two, isn't it?" he exclaimed in utter amazement! He seemed a little stunned but when he had recovered he shook their hands and congratulated them. They still couldn't quite take it all in.

"There are all the coaches," declared Adam confidently.
"But which one is ours?" said Ben.
There were so many coaches that it was difficult to see which was theirs.

They walked past several coaches until Adam thought he recognised one. It was nearly opposite the church, but quite near to a road junction.
"There are lots of coaches but I don't think that any should have parked quite so close to that junction," said Ben critically.
"I guess it's the only time in the year that it's allowed," retorted Adam. "The town is quite

87

small and I guess they have to use every available space."

"Let's cross over and see if it's ours," said Ben.

"Yes," responded Adam, "but we'll walk back away from the junction so that we only have to concentrate on vehicles travelling along this road, and not have to worry about the cars from the other roads as well."

"Now that sounds more like my sensible friend!" smiled Ben.

They retraced their steps a little, moving away from the junction.

"The road seems very busy all of a sudden," said Ben.

"Yes," said Adam, "we will just have to be patient and wait."

They kept looking and listening for traffic. After a little while the road became clear and it was safe for them to cross the road. They checked the road again and saw that it was still safe to cross and so they walked straight across the road looking and listening as they went safely across to the pavement on the other side.

"There you are!" said Ben's mother, obviously relieved to see them both.

"We were so worried when we lost you in the crowds," said Adam's Mother.

"But you'd given us the name of the road, and we asked a policeman for directions, so we were quite safe really," said Adam, feeling rather pleased with himself that they *had* actually found the coach.

"Well done!" said Ben's mother. "You are both very sensible and we are very proud of you. Ben, why didn't you call us?"

Before Ben answered he rather conceitedly

gave his Mother the newspaper.

"What's this?" said his Mother. "You seem to have made headline news! What have you been up to? I hope you've behaved yourselves."

"We've been given two tickets for the National Road-user Activity Centre," said Ben as he held out the tickets for his Mother to see.

"That's wonderful," cried his Mother as she gave him a hug, "Well done!"

The girls were now looking at the paper.

"Well I never!" voiced Rachel. "I guess that Ben answered most of the questions as I'm sure you wouldn't get everything right, Adam."

"Now let's not have any arguments," said her Mother. "We mustn't be jealous."

The coach driver wanted to leave, and he asked everyone to sit down in their seats.

After he had made sure that everyone was on

PARISH CHURCH OF ST. PAUL
TRAVEL
EVENING NEWS
ADAM & BEN: WINNERS

the coach, he closed the door and began to manoeuvre out into the road. The newspaper was being passed around and everyone was congratulating Ben and Adam who related their story in full to the eager listeners.

Adam and Ben planned what they would do when they went back to school: they would show Mrs Williams the newspaper report, and would ask her to teach them lots of different things: marching out of assembly, circus acts, clowning activities, helping them to make coracles, organising a lot of road-user activities and combining all these with a carnival for the whole school!

Their Mothers were wondering how Mrs Williams would react to their requests! But they were sure that the school would have special lessons learning all about crossing the road safely.

They certainly would have something to write about – maybe they would write an article for the school magazine about their day at the carnival? At least Adam seemed keen to write, something he wasn't normally eager to do!

As Adam lay down in his bed that night, he dreamed about their visit to the Road User Activity Centre and the fantastic day they'd had today and told himself that never again would he protest at having to go to a flower carnival!

Roadwise Educational Publishers exists to teach and encourage pedestrians (especially children) to make wise choices of where to cross a road and how to cross a road safely being aware and alert of the unexpected.

This book is based on 5 alive, (the Road Ed Code for crossing the road). 5 alive is fully explained (how to use hand to remember code) in the 5 alive Skills and Activity Books.

For more information log on to:
www.5alive.org.uk

Jean Roberts first became concerned about accidents to children on the road when a friend's daughter was killed. So, in memory of Helen, and to all children and everyone reading this book we hope that you will be safe when crossing a road.

Thank you to everyone who has been involved in the production of this book, the children, schools and numerous individuals.

Other books in the series:

Let's go to the Balloons
Let's go to the Road-user Activity Centre

5 alive Skills and Activity Books 1-6 include a wide range of activities including making, learning, sorting, research, designing, writing, colouring and working for awards and proficiency certificates.

Log on to
www.5alive.org.uk
for more information